I See a Kookaburra!

DISCOVERING ANIMAL HABITATS AROUND THE WORLD

Steve Jenkins & Robin Page

CLARION BOOKS
AN IMPRINT OF HARPERCOLLINS*PUBLISHERS*
BOSTON   NEW YORK

For Jamie, Alec, and Page. — S.J. & R.P.

www.harpercollinschildrens.com

The text was set in Palatino.
The illustrations are collages of cut and torn paper.

The Library of Congress has cataloged the hardcover edition as follows:
Jenkins, Steve, 1952–
I see a kookaburra!: discovering animal habitats around the
world/by Steve Jenkins and Robin Page.
p. cm.
1. Habitat (Ecology)—Juvenile literature. I. Page, Robin, 1957– II. Title.
QH541.14.J442005
591.7—dc22
2004013188

Designed by Robin Page

ISBN: 978-0-618-50764-1 hardcover
ISBN: 978-0-544-80973-4 paperback

Manufactured in Malaysia
23 RRDA 15 14 13 12

corching deserts and steamy rain forests, muddy ponds and salty oceans — animals are found almost every place on earth. They thrive in all these habitats because, over many generations, animals adapt. They change their size, shape, and habits to fit different conditions. Where there's not much water, they are able to use every drop. If there are fierce predators on the ground, many animals live in the trees. All over the world, animals have developed different ways of surviving.

Six different parts of the world are shown in this book. Each habitat includes eight of the animals that live there. Just like real animals, they may be difficult to spot at first. See if you can find them all, then turn the page. You can learn more about these animals at the back of the book.

There are thousands of different kinds of ants. They live almost everywhere on earth and can be found in each of the habitats shown in this book. Along with the eight animals in each picture, there is an ant — somewhere. Can you see it?

In the desert
I see . . .

This desert is in the American Southwest.

. . . a sharp-eyed
kit fox
leaving
its burrow.

. . . a **long-
nosed bat** sipping
nectar from a flower.

. . . an angry
**diamondback
rattlesnake**
buzzing a
warning.

. . . a **trapdoor spider** waiting patiently
in its tunnel.

. . . a tiny **elf owl** making

its nest in a giant cactus.

. . . a **javelina** sniffing out tender roots.

. . . a **kangaroo rat** bounding over the sand.

. . . a poisonous
Gila monster
creeping
slowly over
the rocks.

In a tide pool I see . . .

This tide pool is on the southern coast of England.

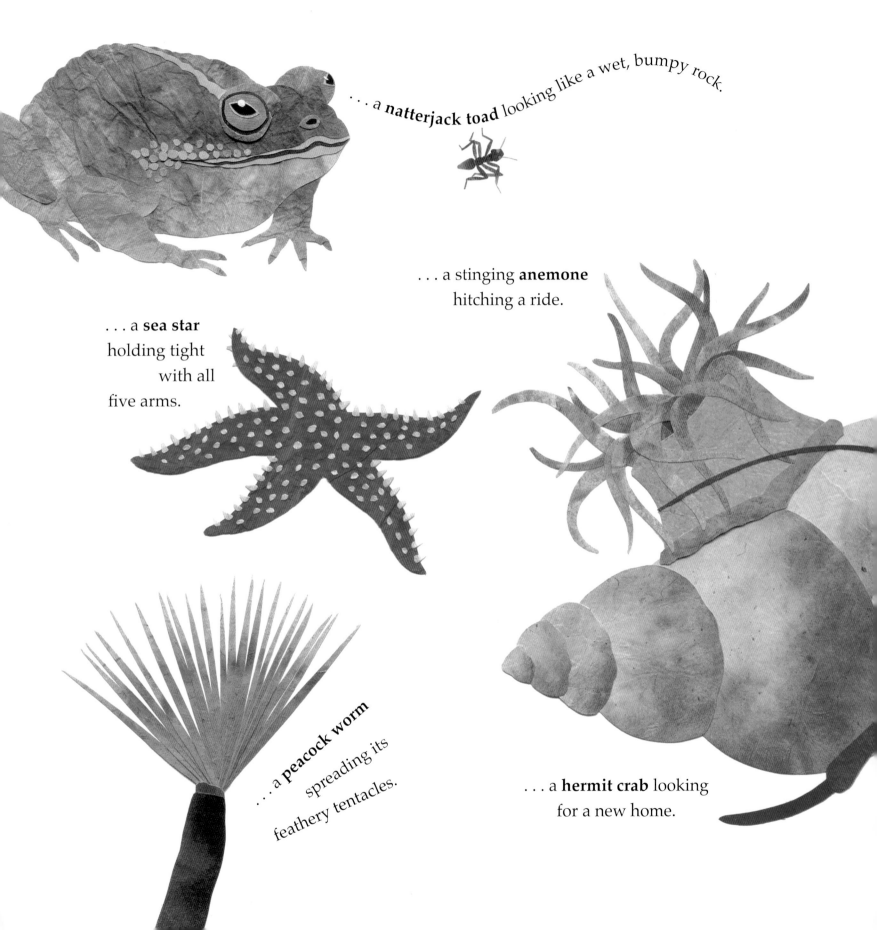

. . . a **natterjack toad** looking like a wet, bumpy rock.

. . . a stinging **anemone** hitching a ride.

. . . a **sea star** holding tight with all five arms.

. . . a **peacock worm** spreading its feathery tentacles.

. . . a **hermit crab** looking for a new home.

. . . a hungry **oystercatcher** searching for a juicy shellfish.

. . . a **sea urchin**, a colorful pincushion.

. . . a poisonous **weever fish** waiting for its next meal.

In the jungle I see . . .

This jungle, or rain forest, is in the Amazon River basin of South America.

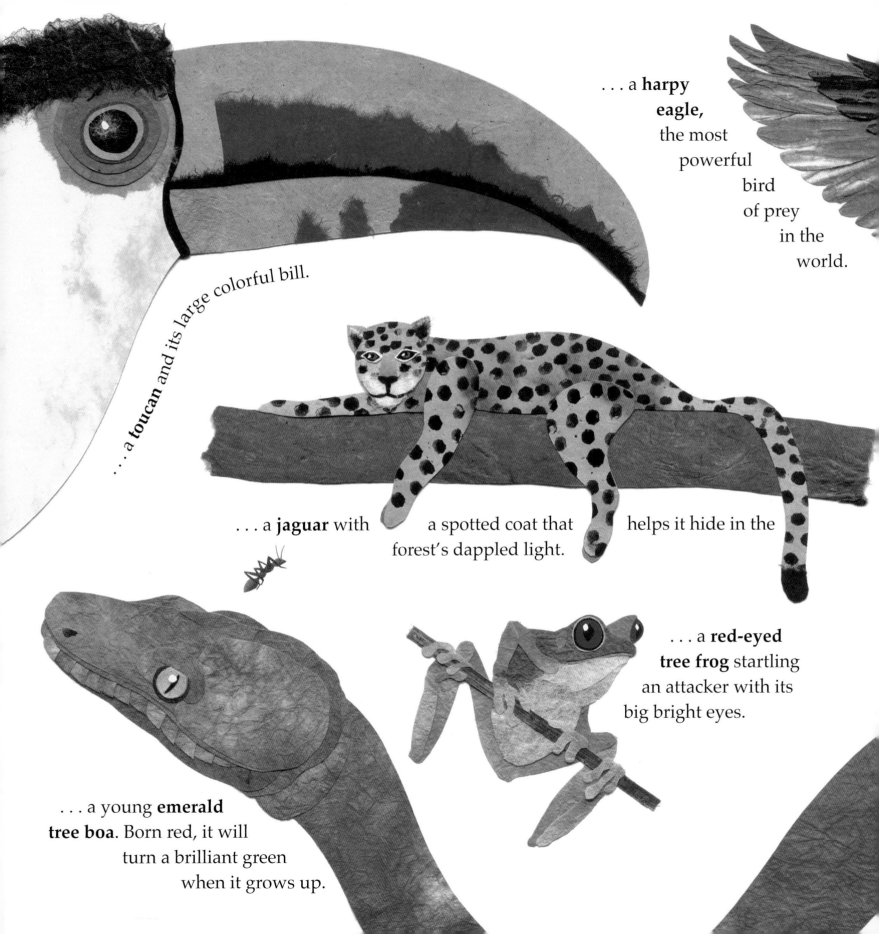

. . . a **harpy eagle,** the most powerful bird of prey in the world.

. . . a **toucan** and its large colorful bill.

. . . a **jaguar** with a spotted coat that helps it hide in the forest's dappled light.

. . . a **red-eyed tree frog** startling an attacker with its big bright eyes.

. . . a young **emerald tree boa**. Born red, it will turn a brilliant green when it grows up.

. . . a **rhinoceros beetle,**
the world's strongest insect.

. . . a
**spider
monkey**
escaping
danger by
swinging
from
branch to
branch.

. . . the fierce-looking but timid **green iguana.**

On the savanna
I see . . .

This savanna, or grassland, is in central Africa.

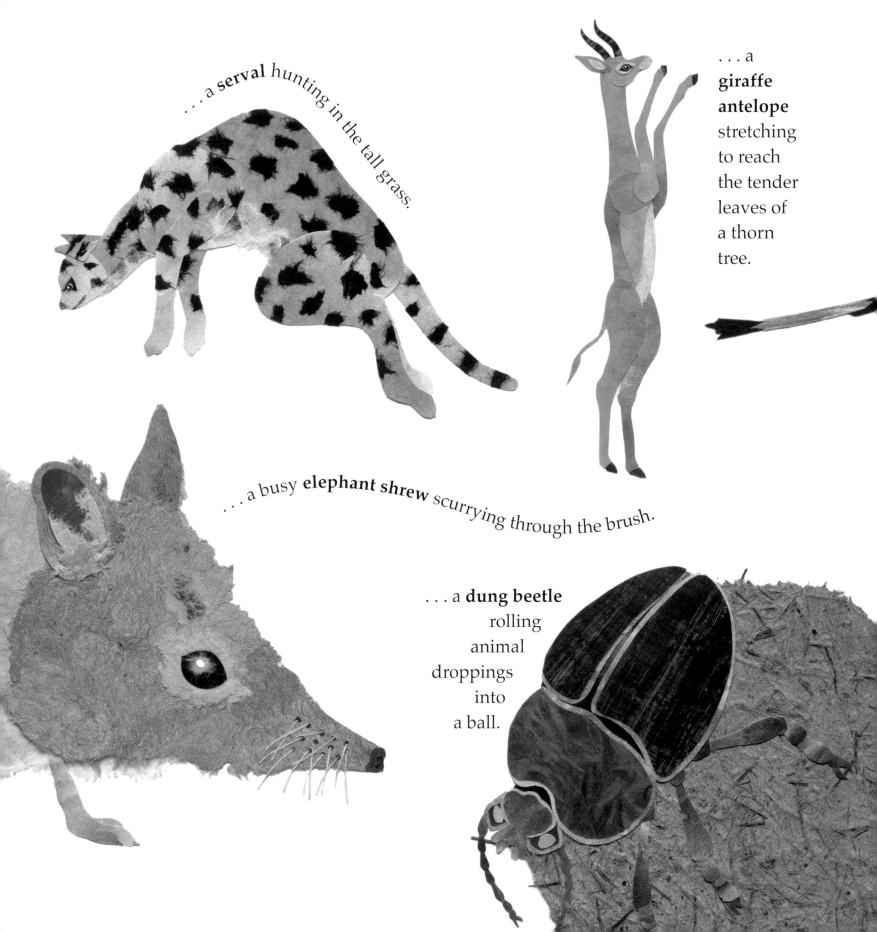

. . . a **serval** hunting in the tall grass.

. . . a **giraffe antelope** stretching to reach the tender leaves of a thorn tree.

. . . a busy **elephant shrew** scurrying through the brush.

. . . a **dung beetle** rolling animal droppings into a ball.

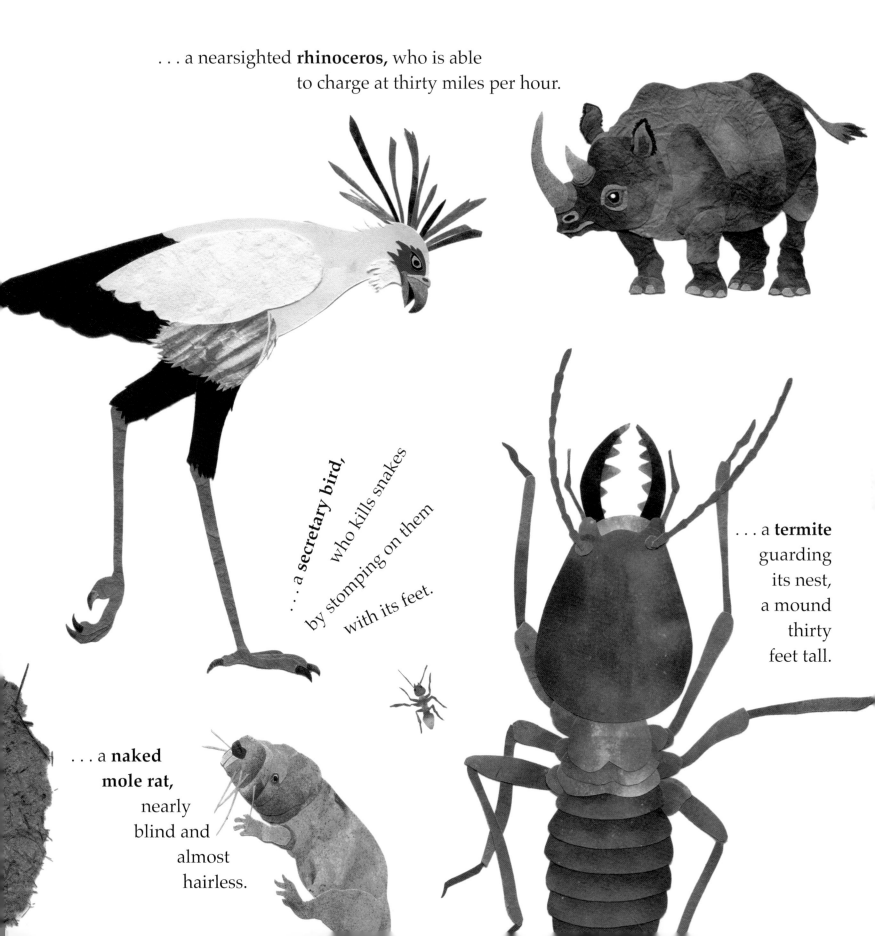

. . . a nearsighted **rhinoceros,** who is able
to charge at thirty miles per hour.

. . . a **secretary bird,**
who kills snakes
by stomping on them
with its feet.

. . . a **termite**
guarding
its nest,
a mound
thirty
feet tall.

. . . a **naked
mole rat,**
nearly
blind and
almost
hairless.

In the forest
I see . . .

This forest is in eastern Australia.

. . . a noisy **kookaburra,** with a call that sounds like crazy laughter.

. . . a **cicada,** a bug that spends its first seven years living underground.

. . . a **dingo,** a fierce wild dog on the hunt.

. . . a **frilled lizard** startling an attacker.

. . . a furry **koala** fast asleep.

. . . a **walking stick insect** hiding in plain sight.

. . . a **cassowary**, a huge flightless bird with a "helmet" on its head.

. . . an **echidna**, a prickly, egg-laying mammal.

In a pond I see . . .

This pond is in the American Midwest.

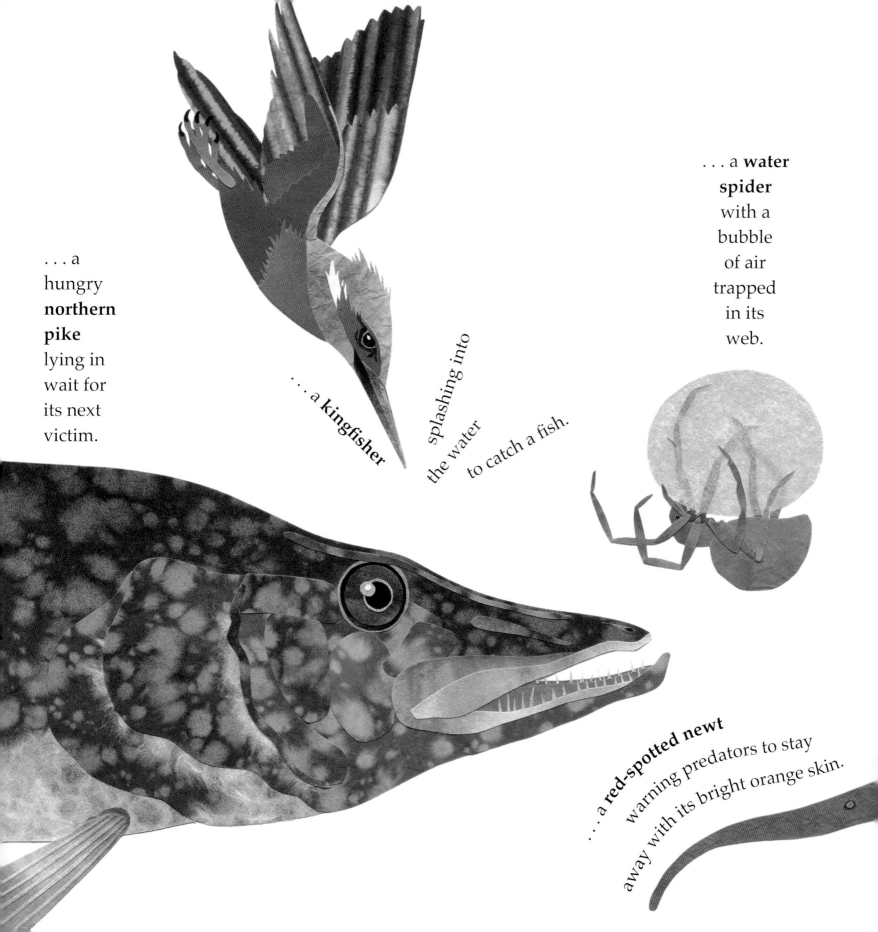

. . . a hungry **northern pike** lying in wait for its next victim.

. . . a **kingfisher** splashing into the water to catch a fish.

. . . a **water spider** with a bubble of air trapped in its web.

. . . a **red-spotted newt** warning predators to stay away with its bright orange skin.

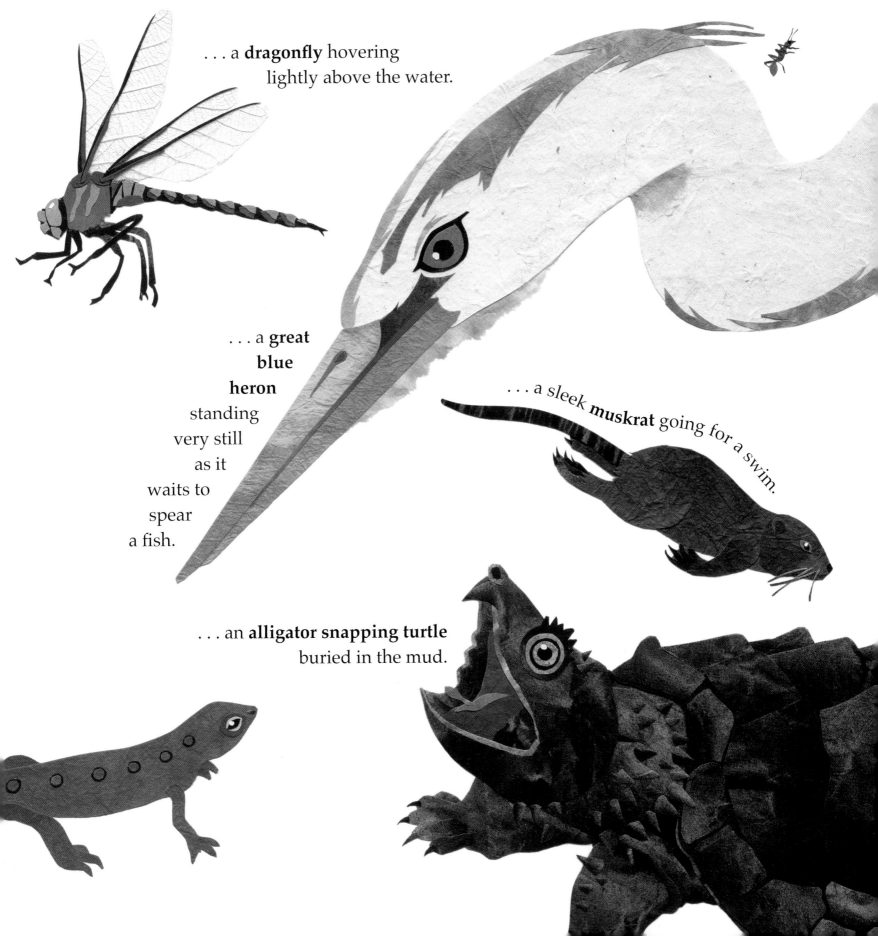

. . . a **dragonfly** hovering
lightly above the water.

. . . a **great
blue
heron**
standing
very still
as it
waits to
spear
a fish.

. . . a sleek **muskrat** going for a swim.

. . . an **alligator snapping turtle**
buried in the mud.

DESERT

In the desert it almost never rains or snows. Deserts can be hot or cold, but they are always dry. The desert shown in this book, in the American Southwest, has daytime temperatures in the summer of well over 100 degrees Fahrenheit. Many of the animals that live here rest during the middle of the day and are active in the cooler morning and evening. Others come out only at night. Desert animals are able to get along with very little water. A few don't drink at all — they get the water they need from their food.

 The **kit fox** is small, about the size of a housecat, with a big bushy tail. It leaves its underground burrow in the evening and hunts through the night. The kit fox has very sensitive hearing, and uses its big ears to detect mice and other small animals moving in the dark. This fox eats rabbits, mice, lizards, insects, and even berries. It can move very swiftly over short distances, and either runs down its prey or lies in wait and pounces.

 The **lesser long-nosed bat** eats only nectar and fruit. It feeds on the flowers of several different kinds of cactus and helps these plants reproduce by carrying pollen from one plant to another. This bat has a wingspan of about six inches and weighs less than one ounce. Lesser long-nosed bats roost in large colonies in caves and old mines, and they come out at sunset to feed.

 The **trapdoor spider**, about one inch long, is a master of construction and disguise. It digs a hole with its fangs, lines it with the fine silk of its web, and then makes a perfectly fitting hinged door of silk and dirt. When this door is closed, it's almost impossible to detect. The trapdoor spider hunts by sitting in its tunnel with the door open slightly. When an insect comes close, the spider runs out, grabs its prey, and drags it back to its underground tunnel. The spider makes two holes on the underside of the door so that it can grasp the door with its fangs, holding it closed against any intruder.

 The **diamondback rattlesnake** can be more than six feet long. The rattlesnake has a reputation of being a frightening, aggressive animal. In fact, it is nervous and shy. Like most snakes, it usually won't bite a person unless it is picked up or stepped on, but its poison is very painful and can be deadly. The rattlesnake is a pit viper — it has heat-sensitive pits on its face that it uses to detect the mice, rabbits, and other small mammals that it eats. The snake's rattle, which is made of the same substance as our fingernails, is used to warn away predators. A ring, or rattle, is added each time the snake sheds its skin, which happens three or four times a year.

 Only five and a half inches long, the **elf owl** is the smallest owl. It usually builds its nest in an abandoned woodpecker hole in the giant saguaro cactus. The plant's sharp spines protect the owl and its young from predators. The elf owl eats insects, small mice, and lizards. If threatened, this tiny bird will lie very still, pretending to be dead.

 The **javelina**, or collared peccary, gets its name from its razor-sharp tusks — *javelina* is Spanish for "spear." This relative of the pig stands two feet tall and weighs about fifty pounds. It lives in groups of ten to fifty animals. The javelina has poor eyesight but a very good sense of smell. It can smell tubers, or roots, that are several feet under the ground, then uses its hooves and tusks to dig them up. The javelina eats just about anything, including seeds, nuts, roots, fruit, cacti, insects, and reptiles. This animal has a very strong odor, and is often smelled before it is seen.

 The **kangaroo rat** comes out of its burrow in the evening. It's a small rodent, with a body three or four inches long and a tail that's one and a half times as long as its body. The kangaroo rat hops on its back legs and can move very quickly. It has large furry feet that help it jump in loose, sandy soil. This rat eats seeds and grasses, and can go its entire life without drinking water.

 There are just two poisonous lizards in the world. One of them is the brightly colored **Gila monster** (the other is the Mexican beaded lizard). The Gila monster is about twenty inches long and weighs about three pounds. The slow-moving Gila monster eats bird eggs and sometimes baby rats or rabbits. This lizard can store fat in its tail. During the winter it stays in its burrow and can go for months without eating.

TIDE POOL

Tide pools are found along rocky sea coasts all over the world. At low tide, a tide pool is higher than the waves. The water is calm, and animals can move about and feed, though they have to be careful not to be eaten themselves. At high tide, waves crash over the tide pool and the animals who live there have to leave or hold on tightly so that they're not smashed into the rocks or washed away.

 The **natterjack toad** doesn't live in the tide pool. It makes its home in sandy, grassy areas near the coast and visits the tide pool to feed on the insects crawling over the rocks at low tide. Natterjack toads are small, only about three inches long. They have shorter legs than other toads, and they don't jump or hop. Instead, they walk and run like a mouse.

 Sea stars, also called starfish, come in many shapes, sizes, and colors. Most are six to twelve inches across, but a few can reach three feet in width. They have from five to twenty-four arms. These arms are bumpy on top and covered on the bottom with thousands of tiny tubelike feet. The sea star eats clams, oysters, and other shellfish. It grips its victim's shell firmly and slowly pulls its two sides apart. Then the sea star pushes its stomach into the animal's shell, digesting the soft shellfish inside. If a sea star loses an arm, it can grow a new one in its place.

The **peacock worm**, which can be twelve inches long, builds a tube by gluing grains of sand together with mucus. It lives inside this tube, which is several inches long and is attached to the bottom of the tide pool. When covered with water, the peacock worm extends its feathery tentacles and filters tiny bits of food from the water. If it is disturbed or exposed at low tide, the worm withdraws completely into its tube.

A **hermit crab** has big, armored claws and a soft, unprotected belly. It lives in the abandoned shell of another animal, carrying its house with it wherever it goes. When it grows too large for its home, it finds a larger shell and quickly moves in. The hermit crab eats both plants and small animals. It, in turn, is eaten by larger crabs, fish, and birds. The hermit crab can grow to be a few inches long. Its relative, the land hermit crab, is a popular pet. The hermit crab has symbiotic, or mutually beneficial, relationships with other animals, like the **anemone**. Some anemones live only on hermit crab shells. They eat bits of food stirred up by the crab as it feeds and moves around. In return, their poisonous tentacles help protect the hermit crab from its enemies.

The **oystercatcher** is a big wading bird, almost one and a half feet long. At low tide, it perches on rocks and wades through tide pools, looking for mussels and oysters. Sometimes the oystercatcher can pry open a shell with its sharp beak. If not, it will pick up the shellfish and smash it against a rock until its shell breaks. The oystercatcher's eggs look just like pebbles, which helps protect them from animals that want to eat them.

The **sea urchin** is a relative of the starfish. It moves slowly over the rocks, feeding on plants and algae. The sea urchin's spines, which protect it from predators, can be very painful if they are stepped on or break off in a person's skin. Sea urchins in deep water can measure a foot in diameter, but they are smaller in tide pools — usually just a few inches across.

People who swim or wade in the shallow water of tide pools should avoid the **weever fish**. This fish, which is about six inches long, is a predator. It buries itself in the sand, popping out suddenly to grab smaller fish with its sharp teeth. It's the sharp spines on the fish's back, however, that can be dangerous to people; these spines contain a powerful poison. If someone steps on a weever fish with a bare foot, he or she receives a jab that can cause serious pain and swelling.

JUNGLE

The great Amazon River flows through the largest tropical jungle, or rain forest, in the world. Covering more than one third of South America, the Amazon rain forest is home to nearly half of all known plant and animal species. There are thousands, perhaps millions, of other plants and animals living there that we have not yet discovered. Unfortunately, this forest is being destroyed — cut down for lumber or burned to make farmland — at a rapid rate. If it is not protected, the entire Amazon rain forest and most of the animals that live there could be gone in fifty years.

The **toucan** is a large bird, with a body two feet long. Its huge beak, or bill, is often as long as the rest of its body. The toucan uses its bill, which is strong but very light, to eat fruit and insects. No one is sure why its bill is so large and colorful. Perhaps it is also used to fight, or to signal other toucans in the forest.

The **harpy eagle** is one of the largest eagles, weighing up to twenty pounds. It has very powerful claws for grasping monkeys and sloths that it snatches out of the branches. Because it hunts in thick forests, its wings are shorter than those of most other eagles, allowing it to maneuver between closely spaced trees.

The **jaguar**, which once lived throughout much of the Americas, is found from Mexico to the middle of South America. It is powerfully built, weighing up to three hundred pounds. It's the third largest cat — only the tiger and lion are larger. The jaguar likes to swim and is often found near water. It eats deer, wild pigs, and other large animals, often lying in wait in trees and jumping onto its prey. If it can't find large animals to hunt, it will also eat lizards, turtles, fish, and armadillos.

An adult **emerald boa** can be up to ten feet long and is a bright green color that blends in with the trees where it lives. This coloring camouflages the snake and allows it to sneak up on its prey: birds, small mammals, and lizards. No one is sure why the young boas are red, orange, or yellow — perhaps these colors protect them by making them look like smaller, poisonous snakes that live in the same area. The emerald boa can sense warm-blooded animals, even at night, with a pit on its face that is sensitive to heat.

The **red-eyed tree frog** spends its life in the trees of the rain forest. It lays its eggs in small pools of water that collect in leaves and hollows in the branches. This small frog, two to three inches long, is active at night. It uses its huge eyes to help it find insects. If it's disturbed during the day, its bright red eyes may surprise an attacker and give it time to escape.

The **rhinoceros beetle**, also called a Hercules beetle, is the world's strongest insect. This beetle is huge — with its horn, it can be more than six inches long. It eats rotten fruit and other vegetation. The male uses its horn, which can be longer than the rest of its body, to fight for territory with other males.

The acrobat of the rain forest is the **spider monkey**. It has long, slender arms and legs and its body is about eighteen inches long. Its most remarkable feature, however, is its tail. This tail is longer than the monkey's body and is used as a fifth hand to grab branches or hold food. The spider monkey lives in large groups in the trees and almost never comes down to the ground. It eats mostly fruit but also feeds on leaves, nuts, and insects.

It looks like a dragon and can be seven feet long, but the **green iguana** is shy and gentle. This lizard eats plants and a few insects, and defends itself by holding very still and trying to blend in with its forest background.

SAVANNA

Though much of Africa is covered with scorching deserts or thick jungles, large parts of the continent are savanna — open grassland with a few scattered trees. This landscape is home to giraffes, zebras, elephants, lions, cheetahs, and thousands of other animals.

The **serval** stands quietly, using its large ears to listen for small animals moving in the grass. Then it leaps high into the air and pounces on its prey. A large serval can be forty inches long and weigh up to twenty pounds. It has the longest legs, for its size, of any cat.

The **giraffe antelope**, also called a gerenuk, is shy and graceful. It stands three or four feet tall at the shoulder, but standing on its back legs and stretching out its long neck, it can reach leaves eight feet off the ground. Its long legs are designed for reaching rather than running, and this antelope is not a fast runner. When frightened, it tries to sneak away quietly, keeping close to the ground. The gerenuk never has to drink. It gets all the water it needs from the plants it eats.

The **elephant shrew** can be twelve inches long and weigh one and a half pounds — about the size of a rabbit. Though it looks like a rodent, the elephant shrew belongs to an ancient group of animals and is not closely related to any other mammal. It uses its keen eyesight, hearing, and sense of smell to avoid predators and find insects, which it catches and eats with its long, flexible snout. This animal has long legs and can move very quickly. It runs back and forth constantly on a complex system of trails that it makes in the grass. It keeps these trails neat and clean and fights furiously with other elephant shrews that invade its territory.

Dung beetles are one of the most important animals of the savanna. Without them, the grassland would soon be buried in the droppings of large grazing animals. Dung beetles are found all over the world, but the ones living on the African plains are the largest, growing up to two inches long. When an elephant or other large plant-eating animal leaves its dung on the ground, thousands of these beetles quickly arrive on the scene. First a beetle cuts off a small piece of dung. Then it stands on its front legs, pushes with its back feet, and rolls the ball of dung to its underground burrow. There the dung provides food and a place for the female beetle to lay her eggs.

There are two different kinds of **rhinoceros** in Africa. Both are endangered. The white rhino, shown here, is really a dark gray color. It is more common than its critically endangered relative the black rhinoceros. These rhinos are hunted for their horns, which some people mistakenly believe contain powerful medicine. The rhinoceros is the second largest land animal (the elephant is bigger), measuring up to thirteen feet in length and weighing five thousand pounds, as much as a pickup truck. Despite their size and weight, these plant-eating animals are agile and can run at thirty miles per hour. They have very poor eyesight and will often charge to defend themselves if they are approached. Rhinos like to roll in the mud, which helps protect their tough-looking but sensitive skin from insects and sunburn.

Long ago, secretaries in England were men who wore long wigs and wrote with pens made from quills, or hollow feathers. Sometimes they stuck these pens into their wigs to keep them handy. When explorers saw a large bird with feathers sticking out of its head like quill pens, they named it the **secretary bird**. This bird, which stands four feet tall, often hunts in pairs. It eats snakes, lizards, and small mammals, killing them with hard kicks of its strong feet.

African **termites** live in colonies that can contain millions of insects. They eat decaying wood and plants and build rock-hard mounds, which are made of soil mixed with saliva. These mounds can be more than thirty feet tall. When a mound is abandoned by a termite colony, it often becomes a home for small mammals, birds, and reptiles. Each colony contains a queen termite. The queen is enormous — up to five inches long — and can lay 30,000 eggs a day. In some parts of the world, people eat termite queens as a delicacy.

The **naked mole rat** is the only mammal that lives in colonies like those of ants, bees, and termites. An underground mole rat colony may contain more than one hundred animals. Each colony includes a queen, who gives birth to all the young, along with soldier mole rats and worker mole rats. These small rodents, about three inches long and weighing one or two ounces, are almost hairless and nearly blind. They eat the roots of plants and can seriously damage farmers' crops. A single colony of naked mole rats may build and use more than two miles of tunnels.

FOREST

Much of Australia is covered by a hot, sandy desert. Other parts of the continent are lush, tropical rain forest. This Australian forest is another kind of environment. There are trees and shrubs and moderate rainfall, and it's not too hot or cold. It's a lot like forests in many other parts of the world, except that many of the plants and animals here are found nowhere else. Australia has been an island for millions of years, and many living things here developed in unique ways.

As the sun comes up, the **kookaburra** greets the new day with a call that sounds like loud, crazy laughter. The kookaburra is a large bird, about eighteen inches long. It eats snakes, lizards, and other birds, and practices an unusual hunting technique. After catching a snake, it flies up into the air and kills its prey by dropping it from a great height.

The **cicada** spends most of its life underground as a nymph, or immature insect. It feeds on sap in tree roots and slowly grows until, after seven years, it emerges as an adult with millions of other cicadas. This part of a cicada's life is short — only a few weeks. When above ground, cicadas live in trees and are known for the loud chirping calls they use to attract their mates.

About 3,500 years ago people brought the first dogs to Australia, probably from India. When they reached Australia, many these dogs ran away, became wild, and soon spread across the continent. Known as **dingoes,** some of these wild dogs were tamed by the aborigines, the original native people of Australia, but many others have remained wild. The dingo is a medium-size dog, averaging about thirty pounds. It is a fierce predator who hunts in packs, and it has greatly reduced or wiped out many of the native birds and marsupial mammals. The dingo growls, whines, and howls but cannot bark.

The **frilled lizard** is about eight inches long. It spends most of its time in trees, where it eats insects and small lizards. When frightened, this reptile can startle an attacker by opening a large frill of skin around its neck that is more than twelve inches across. If this tactic fails, the frilled lizard can stand up and run away on its back legs. It is nicknamed the "bicycle lizard."

Koalas are not bears. They are marsupials, animals that raise their young in a pouch, and are related to kangaroos. Koalas eat the leaves of just one kind of tree, the eucalyptus. They get most of the water they need from these leaves, and they rarely drink. Eucalyptus leaves are not very nutritious, so koalas save energy by sleeping twenty hours a day. A full-grown koala weighs fifteen to twenty pounds.

The **cassowary** is the second-largest bird in the world, smaller only than the ostrich. It stands six and a half feet tall and weighs as much as 180 pounds. The hard crest on this bird's head protects it as it pushes through the thick undergrowth of the forest. The cassowary is a gentle creature that eats seeds and fruit, but if attacked it can defend itself with long, sharp claws and fierce kicks. A cassowary can kill a grown man with its feet. The male cassowary has the job of sitting on the eggs and raising the young birds when they hatch. There are only about 1,500 cassowaries left in the wild, making this one of the world's most endangered animals.

Walking stick insects are found in many parts of the world, and some of the largest live in Australia. The **Titan walking stick insect** is up to ten inches long. It eats the leaves of trees and shrubs and is rarely seen because of its excellent camouflage. When disturbed, the walking stick insect goes rigid and sways back and forth in the breeze, making itself look even more like a stick or twig.

The **echidna,** one of the few egg-laying mammals, is also called a spiny anteater. It is a member of a very ancient group of mammals. Echidnas, or animals a lot like them, have probably been around for 100 million years. The echidna is about the size of a housecat. It eats termites and ants, tearing open their nests with sharp claws and slurping up the insects with a long, sticky tongue. An echidna has the unusual ability to detect very faint electric fields with its nose. Since all living things produce a small electric current, the echidna can use its nose to locate insects moving underground.

POND

Ponds are depressions in the ground, either natural or man-made, that hold water throughout the year. They are smaller than lakes and are usually surrounded by plants. They provide homes, water, and food for many different animals.

The **northern pike** is a fast and powerful predator. It lies motionless among rocks and weeds, then darts out to seize a passing fish in its sharp, backward-pointing teeth. It also eats frogs, ducklings, and mammals that swim or fall into the water. The pike has special motion-detecting sensors on its head and along the side of its body that help it find prey in muddy water. The largest northern pike ever caught weighed more than forty-six pounds, but most of these fish aren't more than three feet in length and about twenty pounds in weight.

The **kingfisher** sits on a perch over the water. When it spots a fish, it hovers as high as fifty feet in the air, then folds its wings and dives straight into the water. When a kingfisher catches a fish, it will beat it on a rock or tree to stun it, then flip it into the air and swallow it head first. This bird will also eat frogs, insects, and crayfish. Kingfishers are large birds, twelve or thirteen inches long. They don't build their nests in trees. Instead, they make their homes at the end of long tunnels they dig into dirt banks.

The **water spider**, about one inch long, spins a net of silk under water. It fills this net with tiny air bubbles brought from the surface. Soon it has a large underwater home filled with air. It catches and poisons insects and tiny fish in the water and takes them into its air chamber, storing them to eat later.

The **red-spotted newt** is an amphibian. It spends part of its life on land and part in the water, but it can adapt from one environment to the other if, for example, a pond dries up. This newt is four or five inches long. When living in water, it is a vivid orange color. This is a warning to predators, because the red-spotted newt's skin contains poison that most animals want to avoid. Newts eat insects, worms, and tadpoles.

The **dragonfly** is a swift, acrobatic hunter. It can fly faster than thirty miles per hour and holds the speed record of the insect world. A dragonfly can hover, fly sideways, and even fly backwards. It hunts flying insects, including other dragonflies, catching them in the air and killing them with its strong jaws. The largest living dragonfly has wings about six inches across. Dragonflies have been around for hundreds of millions of years, and at one time had wingspans of two and a half feet.

The **great blue heron** is a long-legged wading bird. A large bird, it stands four feet tall and has a wingspan of six feet. This bird is found along the shores of both freshwater ponds and rivers and saltwater bays and marshes. It hunts by walking slowly through shallow water or standing in one spot, as still as a statue. The great blue heron holds its long graceful neck coiled in an S shape until it spots a fish, snake, frog, or other small animal. Then it strikes quickly with its long pointed bill, spearing its prey.

Like the beaver, the **muskrat** is a rodent that spends most of its time in the water. The muskrat has a body about twelve inches long, with a hairless tail that's flattened at the tip to help the animal swim. It also has webbed back feet and oily waterproof fur that keeps it warm in cold water. The muskrat makes its home in mud banks or in piles of sticks in the water. It eats water plants, as well as fish and frogs. In the past, muskrats were trapped for their fur, but they are not endangered.

The **alligator snapping turtle** is a huge reptile, sometimes weighing more than 200 pounds, with a shell up to thirty inches long. To find food, this turtle buries itself in the mud at the bottom of a pond. Then it wriggles a small, pink wormlike growth on the bottom of its open mouth. When a fish, frog, or other turtle comes to investigate, the snapper closes its powerful jaws, catching its next meal. This turtle also eats plants and dead animals in the water. A snapping turtle breathes air but can hold its breath for up to fifty minutes. If caught, it must be handled carefully, as it is short-tempered and can easily take off a person's finger with its sharp beak.

Ants are found everywhere on earth except for the polar regions and a few islands. Almost nine thousand different kinds of ants have been named, and there are probably thousands more. Ants are social insects — they live in colonies that can contain thousands of individuals. These colonies build complex nests underground or in hollow trees. Each ant in a colony has a special job. There are worker ants, soldier ants, and ants that take care of the queen, who lays all of the colony's eggs.

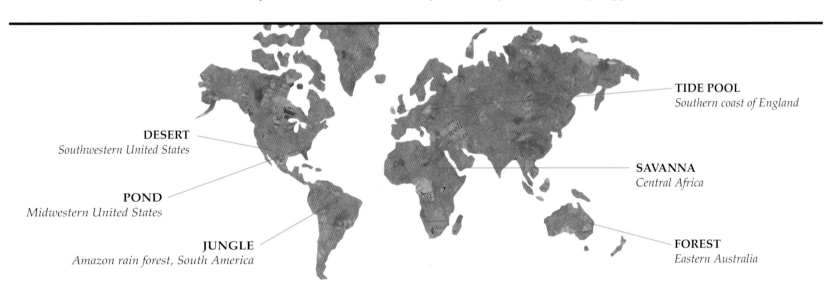

TIDE POOL
Southern coast of England

DESERT
Southwestern United States

SAVANNA
Central Africa

POND
Midwestern United States

JUNGLE
Amazon rain forest, South America

FOREST
Eastern Australia

ADDITIONAL READING

Burnie, David, and Don E. Wilson, eds. *Animal.* New York: Smithsonian Institution, 2001.

Findley, Rowe. *Great American Deserts.* New York: Simon and Schuster, 1972.

Groves, Colin. *Animal Kingdom.* New York: Barnes and Noble Books, 2001.

Rees, Robin, et al. *The Way Nature Works.* New York: Macmillan, 1992.

Tayler, Barbara. *The Animal Atlas.* New York: Random House, 1992.

Winston, Peggy. *Explore a Tropical Forest.* Washington, D.C.: National Geographic Society, 1989.